OUTSIDE AND INSIDE

SHARKS

BY SANDRA MARKLE

SCHOLASTIC INC.

New York Toronto London Auckland Sydney

For Diana Massengale, whose friendship helps me
survive swimming with the sharks

The author would like to thank Dr. Wesley R. Strong, marine biologist, University of California, Santa Barbara; Dr. H. Wesley Pratt, University of Rhode Island National Oceanic and Atmospheric Administration Fisheries; Dr. Edward Hodgson, Tufts University; Dr. Seymour Zigman, Department of Ophthalmology, University of Rochester Medical Center; Dr. Sanford Moss, University of Massachusetts, North Dartmouth; Hera Konstantinou, Department of Wildlife and Fisheries, Texas A&M University; and Dr. Adrianus Kalmijn, Scripps Oceanographic Institution, for sharing their expertise and enthusiasm.

ISBN 0-590-02653-4

20 19 18 17 16   6 7 8 9/0

Printed in the U.S.A.   08

First Scholastic printing, September 1998

Book design by Anne Scatto/ PIXEL PRESS
The text of this book is set in 16 pt Melior.

NOTE: To help readers pronounce words that may not be familiar to them, there is a pronunciation guide on page 37. These words are italicized the first time they appear.

TITLE PAGE: *Gray reef shark*

Sharks are awesome! Would you believe that a shark can locate an animal hiding under the sand on the sea bottom? Or that it can track down a wounded animal too far away to be seen? How can a shark do those things? And why do some sharks that are bigger than a city bus have teeth so tiny they're almost invisible? What do these shark giants eat? This book will let you explore all these questions and more. You'll even take a peek inside a shark as you learn its secrets.

REEF SHARK

GILL SLITS

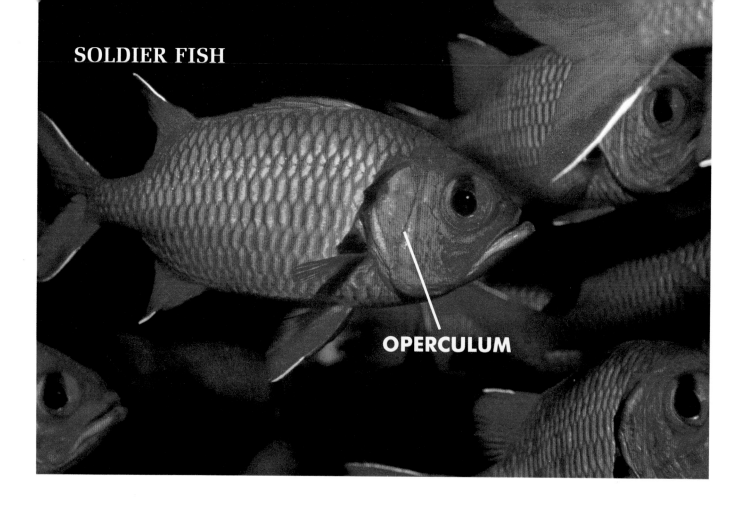

SOLDIER FISH

OPERCULUM

Look at the reef shark and the soldier fish. They are both fish. They both need *oxygen,* a gas in air and water, to live. And they both have special body parts called gills that carry oxygen from the water into their bodies. But there are differences between sharks and other fish. A shark's gills are in separate pouches with slits opening to the inside and outside of its body. The soldier fish, and other fish like it, have gills grouped in one chamber covered by a protective plate called the *operculum.*

A shark's tail usually has a top part that is longer than the bottom. Other fish usually have tails with two equal parts. But the biggest difference between sharks and other fish is on the inside.

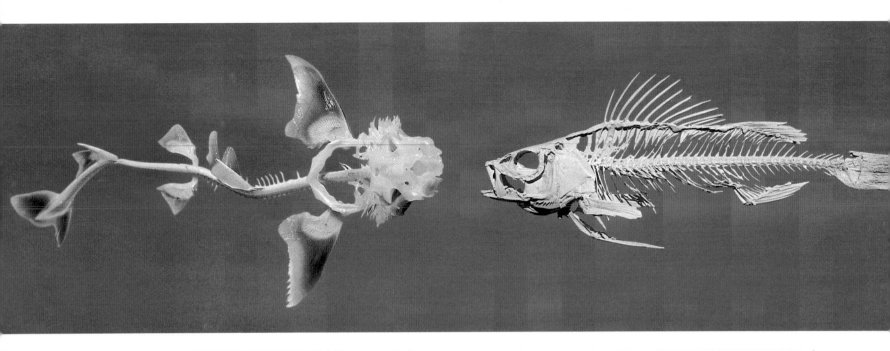

SHARK SKELETON   BONY FISH SKELETON

Like you, all fish have a framework, or *skeleton,* that gives their bodies a shape. Fish, like the soldier fish, that have a skeleton of hard bone are called bony fish. A shark's skeleton isn't made of hard bone. It's made of lightweight, rubbery material called *cartilage.*

Cartilage is still strong, though. Just feel your ear. Its strength and shape come from a cartilage framework. Along a shark's spine and other places where its skeleton needs to be especially strong, the cartilage is reinforced with *calcium,* the material that makes bones hard.

Run a hand down your back. Feel all the bumps? That's your spinal column. This is a piece of the shark's spinal column. It has been stained to reveal the layers of calcium that make it stronger. As a shark gets older, more of these layers are added. So scientists count the layers to guess how long a shark lived. From these studies, they think some sharks may live to be very old—as much as a hundred years old.

BLUE SHARK

DORSAL FINS

CAUDAL FIN

PECTORAL FIN

PELVIC FIN

ANAL FIN

Find this blue shark's caudal, or tail, fin. The fin's side-to-side sweeps propel the shark forward. And the pelvic, anal, and dorsal fins keep the shark from being rolled over by this motion.

A shark moves left and right and up and down by twisting its body and moving its pectoral fins. If you've ever wiggled your hands to help yourself stay afloat while swimming, you can see how moving its fins buoys up the shark in the same way. The shark needs to work to keep from sinking. It lacks a swim bladder, a balloonlike sac, that most bony fish have. Letting oxygen in or out of the swim bladder also allows a bony fish to rise or sink.

Don't worry! This diver was not attacked.
Sharks usually attack only to catch food
or to defend themselves.

A shark's liver helps it float. Look how big the shark's liver is! It's packed with stored body oils. If you've ever seen salad oil poured into water or vinegar, you know oil floats. So the oil-filled liver buoys up the shark, too.

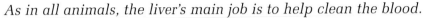

As in all animals, the liver's main job is to help clean the blood.

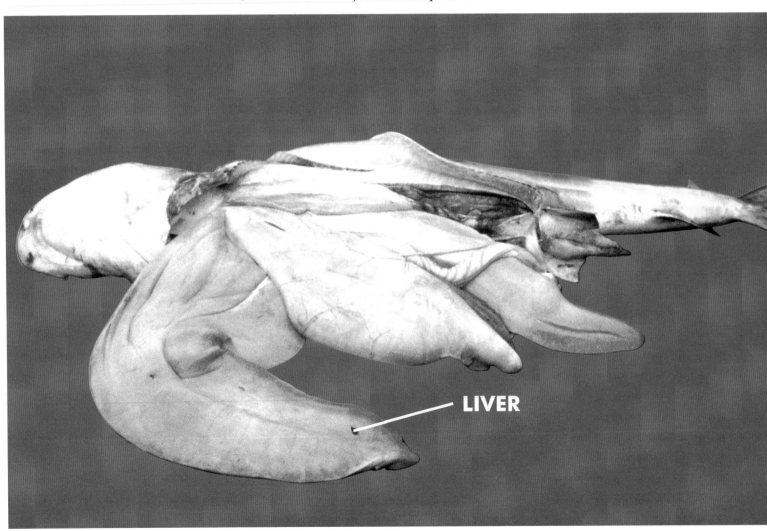

LIVER

Open your mouth and look in a mirror. Your teeth are different shapes—some pointed, some flattened—so you can bite and chew the different types of foods you eat. Similarly, sharks have teeth shaped just right for what they eat. The sand tiger shark on page 12 has curved teeth to snag slippery fish. This great white has large triangular teeth with tiny points along the edges like a steak knife. With these teeth, it easily takes a bite out of even tough-skinned animals.

See the replacement teeth lying flat behind the teeth that are in use?

Can you figure out how this sand tiger shark can close its mouth with all those sharp teeth? Look closely and you'll see the pockets in the jaw that the teeth fit into.

The tooth fairy would go broke paying for a shark's lost teeth! Although a shark generally uses just the front few rows, its mouth may have five or more sets of teeth, one behind the other. Your teeth are firmly set into your jawbone. But a shark's teeth are only loosely anchored in a material that fills a groove in the jaw.

Sharks keep on getting new teeth all their lives. Some shed and replace a set of teeth all at once. But most lose just one or two teeth at a time as the teeth become worn or broken. A loose, old tooth wiggles and even hangs from the gums as a new tooth moves forward to replace it. You may have lost a tooth in this way.

These tooth buds inside the lemon shark's jaw will grow into replacement teeth. Young sharks replace a complete set of teeth about once every two weeks; adult sharks do so about every four to six months.

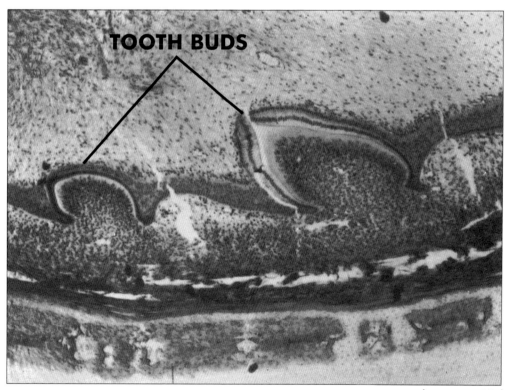

TOOTH BUDS

COMPUTER COLOR-ENHANCED (MAGNIFIED 20X)

13

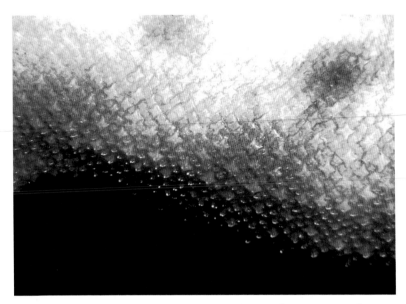

These are a horn shark's denticles. Like your teeth and a shark's teeth, denticles have a soft center pulp with a hard enamel coat.

Sharks even have teethlike scales called *denticles* all over their bodies. These are shed and replaced just like the teeth in their jaws. As they grow bigger, some kinds of sharks add more little denticles to cover their body. Others replace smaller denticles with larger ones.

Denticles on a slow-moving shark, like the whale shark on page 15, are big and tightly packed, forming an armor coat. Denticles on a fast-swimming shark, like the blue shark on page 8, are spread apart and mushroom shaped. Because water slips past these denticles easily, there is little drag to slow the shark down.

Here's a really close look at one marbled shark denticle.

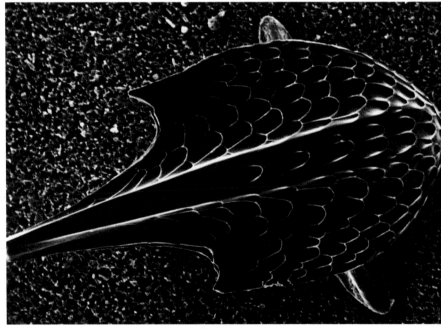

COMPUTER-ENHANCED (MAGNIFIED 200X)

This giant whale shark eats only tiny sea animals called plankton, and small fish like sardines.

So what powers a shark's movements? Its *muscles* do. Usually working in pairs, muscles move individual parts of the skeleton by pulling on them from opposite sides. Waves of muscle action, passing down one side of the shark's body and then the other, swing its tail from side to side. And as the tail pushes against the water, the shark is thrust forward.

This hammerhead shark is hunting for its dinner. All sharks hunt for food—even giant grazers like the whale shark. Some even hunt in the ocean's dark depths or at night. Wonder how a shark finds food? It uses its special senses.

A shark listens. It can hear a wounded animal struggling from as far away as the length of a football field.

The picture below shows you the inside of a blue shark's ear. A shark's ears are fluid-filled canals that connect to small openings on top of its head. What's being lifted out is a soft sac filled with a gritty paste. As the sac moves, tiny hairs touching the walls of the sac bend. This action may trigger signals that travel to the shark's brain on pathways called *nerves*. When the brain figures out the messages, the shark hears. Of course, these events happen almost instantly.

Deep inside the shark's ear are semicircular canals that help it maintain balance. There are also hair-filled parts that sense from what direction sound is coming.

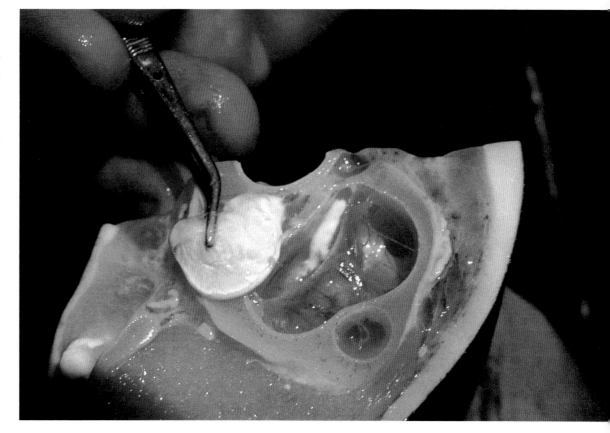

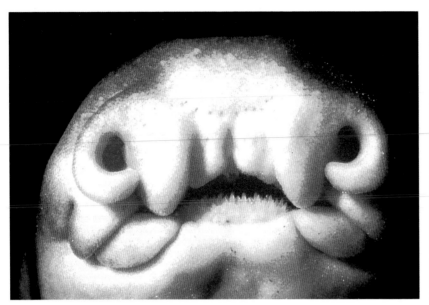

What big nostrils this horn shark has! Horn sharks can smell clams buried in sand or other small animals hidden in caves.

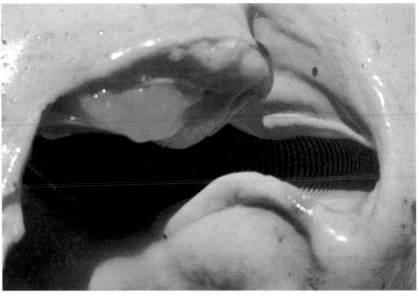

Look at all the folds of tissue inside a lemon shark's nose. The folds allow more smell-sensitive tissue to be packed into a small space.

A shark smells its *prey.* The body juices from a large injured fish can produce an odor trail that sharks sense many meters away. Swimming forces water through a shark's nostrils into its nasal sacs. A shark doesn't breath through its nostrils the way you do. It only smells. Particles in the water cause signals to be sent to the shark's brain.

Because wounded animals are easier prey, sharks are especially attracted to the smell of fresh blood. In fact, a shark can smell as little as five drops of blood mixed into the amount of water it takes to fill an average swimming pool.

When the prey is about as close as two city buses parked end to end, most sharks can see it. Fast-swimming hunters, like the blue shark, usually have better vision than sharks that lie still and ambush prey.

Now, you can see inside a tiger shark's eye. Find the *pupil* and the lens. The pupil is the window that lets light enter. Muscles move the lens forward and back to focus light onto the *retina,* a light-sensitive layer at the back of the eye. Then signals are sent to the shark's brain.

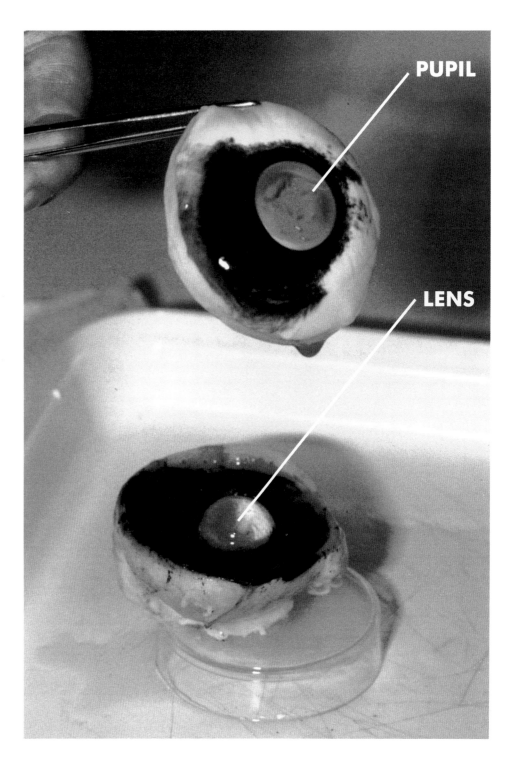

PUPIL

LENS

Look at this frilled shark's eye glow! This eyeshine is caused by a diver's light shining into the shark's eyes and being reflected by a mirrorlike layer. You may have seen an animal's eyes appear to glow this same way when they reflect a car's headlights. The frilled shark lives in the dimly-lit depths. So this reflective layer helps the shark take advantage of what light is available, bouncing it back onto the retina.

This shark, called a wobbegong, is waiting to grab any animal that comes close. Why do you think fish have trouble spotting this shark?

When an animal is close by, a shark feels it move. Wonder how? Next time you're in the bathtub, wiggle one hand in the water. You'll feel the water motion. Fish sense water movement with a system called the lateral line. It's a long tube running down both sides of the body from tail to snout and around each eye. It is connected to the surface by short tubes. Water movement across the openings causes motion in the gelatinlike material inside the tube system. The motion is detected by tiny hairs in the main tube. And they trigger signals that travel to the brain.

Measure a meter from you. When a shark gets about that close it can sense the electricity given off by an animal. It may surprise you to learn that all animals—even you—give off electricity. Tiny charges are produced by each heartbeat or by the movement of any muscle. These charges leak out from openings like an animal's mouth or a fish's gills. A lot of electricity leaks from wounds, making it easier for sharks to find injured animals.

What look like freckles are pores, the openings of the shark's special electricity sensors.

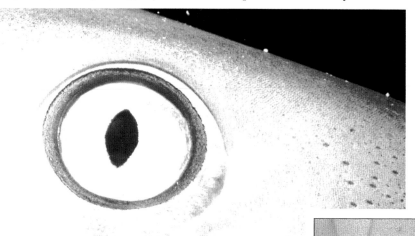

These are the electricity sensors. Researchers think they may also act like a compass, helping a shark know where it is and where it's heading.

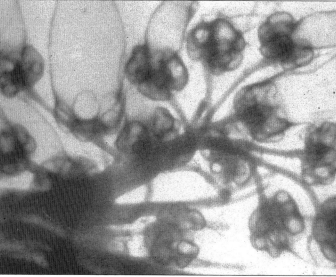

COMPUTER COLOR-ENHANCED (MAGNIFIED 200x)

Take a close look at this blue shark, chomping on a fish. See the lid that has moved up to shield its eye? Most sharks can't blink. But some have a lid that moves up as the shark strikes. Other sharks roll their eyes back to protect them.

Look at this shark's jaws, too. Like most sharks, it has pushed its upper jaw forward and out to bite. You can only move your lower jaw. Some sharks also swing their head from side to side to help their teeth cut out a chunk of their food.

Why do you think this basking shark is swimming along with its big mouth wide open?

Did you guess that the basking shark is catching its dinner? Like the whale shark, it strains tiny plankton from the water. Do you see the light-colored stripes inside the basking shark's mouth? These are its gill arches. Any tiny plankton in the water are trapped in comblike parts that line the gills called gill rakers. And when these gill rakers become clogged with plankton, the shark swallows, pushing the food into its stomach.

These are a basking shark's gill rakers.

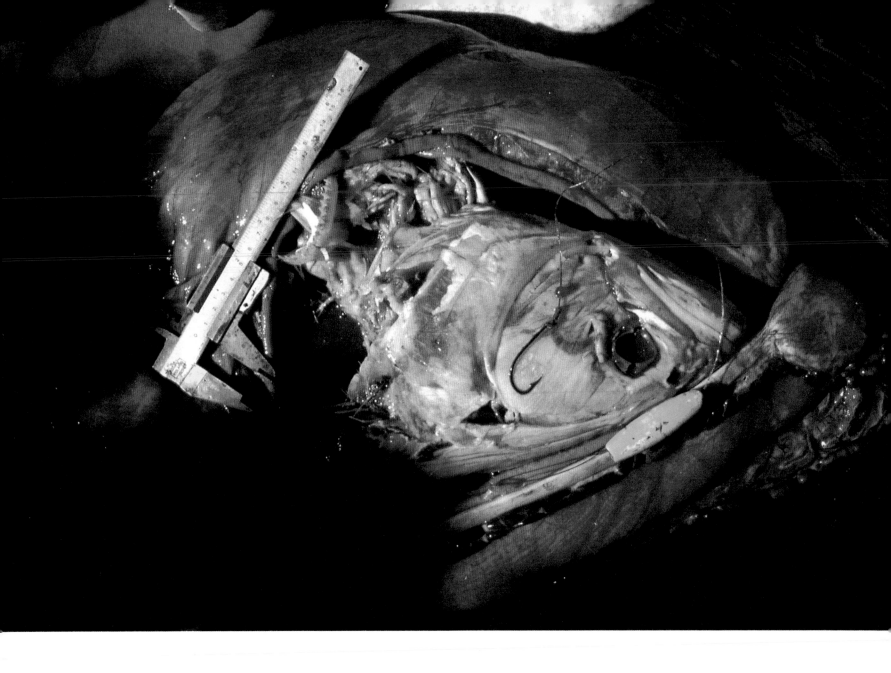

Inside the stomach, muscles and strong juices break even large food into small pieces. Here you can peek inside a mako shark's stomach and see the fish it ate.

Next, the food moves into a tube, the intestine, and more juices attack it. The lower part of the intestine is called the spiral valve because food moves along a spiraling ramp. Here the food is broken down into its basic parts, or *nutrients,* such as proteins and vitamins. And these nutrients pass through the walls and into the blood. The blood carries the nutrients to all parts of the shark's body. Wastes pass out of the shark through an opening between the pelvic fins.

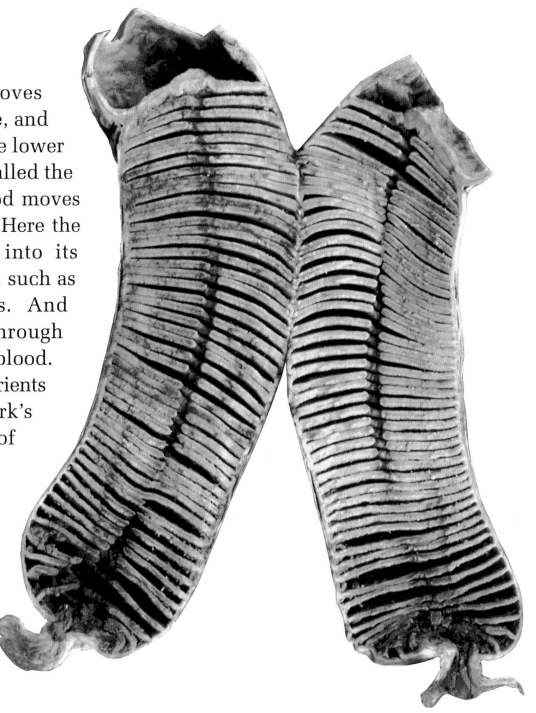

Look inside the spiral valve, which has been cut in half and opened. Its shape allows more nutrients to be collected in a small space.

Besides food, sharks need oxygen to be active. Remember, a shark gets the oxygen it needs from the water through its gills. Some sharks swim openmouthed to force water to flow over the gills. Others can move the lining of their mouth to pump water through the gills.

Water enters mainly through the mouth, flows over the gills, and exits through the gill slits. But some sharks also have a small opening, called the *spiracle,* behind each eye to let water into the gills while the sharks are eating.

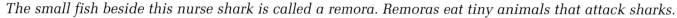

The small fish beside this nurse shark is called a remora. Remoras eat tiny animals that attack sharks.

This is part of a gill. The white part is the supporting arch. Running along it is a tube. And inside that are two more tubes that carry blood to and from the gills. The gill itself is made up of rows of paddlelike parts— each covered by rows of more paddlelike parts. While water is flowing over these gill elements, blood flows through them. And oxygen moves from the water into the blood. Then the blood carries the oxygen to all parts of the shark's body. *Carbon dioxide,* a waste gas given off naturally by the shark's body, passes from the blood through the gills into the water.

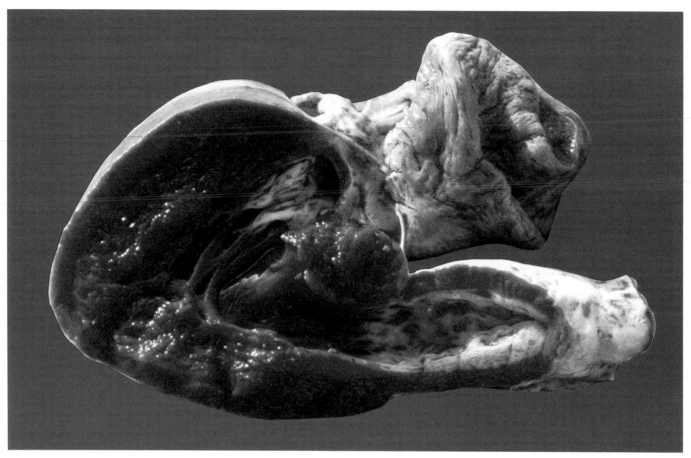

Here you can see inside a mako shark's heart.

So what keeps the blood moving around a shark's body? It's a special muscle, the heart. You have a heart, too, but it's a double pump. One half of your heart sends blood to your lungs, where it picks up oxygen. Then the blood returns and is pumped to the rest of your body by the second pump. The shark's heart is a single pump. It collects blood from the body and sends it to the gills. From there the blood flows on to the rest of the shark's body. And finally the blood returns to the heart.

Perhaps the most important part of a shark's life is having young. When a male shark mates with a female, he uses his pelvic fin to place his sperm into the opening between the female's pelvic fins. The inner parts of the male's pelvic fins form a stiff tube to do this job. Female sharks have a special body part called the shell gland. In most sharks, the male's sperm joins with the female's eggs in the shell gland. Once an egg and a sperm unite, a baby shark begins to develop. In some types of sharks, the shell gland coats the fertilized egg in a tough case. And the female shark lays these eggs.

See the baby cat shark growing inside this egg? Look in the lower left-hand corner. Its body is curled around a ball of yolk, its food supply.

This baby swell shark is just hatching. Its sturdy egg case kept it safe
while it developed. Then, with the help of some extra large denticles, the
baby tore open the egg case.

Here are two baby thresher sharks, each inside its own compartment. Since they are inside the mother's body, each baby's sac is only a thin envelope, unlike the baby swell shark's tough egg case. Around the babies are small eggs packaged by the shell gland. The baby sharks will get the food they need to grow by eating these eggs.

Other types of sharks, like hammerheads, have the baby develop with a cord connecting it to the mother's body. Then food nutrients and oxygen are carried by the mother's blood to the growing baby.

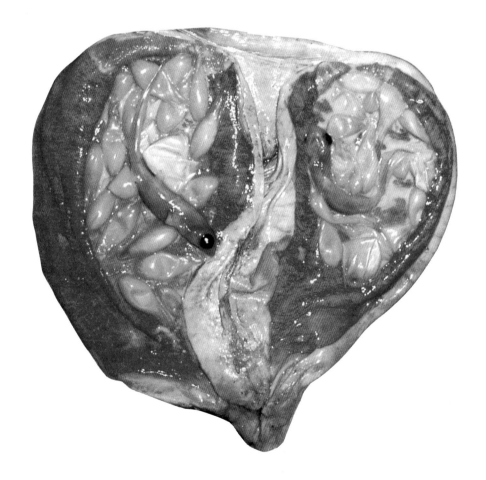

This lemon shark is just being born. After the young shark is completely outside its mother's body, it rests for a few minutes. Then it swims away, breaking the cord.

Whether a baby shark hatches from an egg or leaves its mother's body, it has to take care of itself as soon as it's born. All of its body parts work together to let the young shark stay safe, find food, and grow. And while some sharks grow faster than others, a shark is usually not full grown until it is ten to fifteen years old. Clearly sharks are special . . . from the inside out!

PRONUNCIATION GUIDE

CALCIUM	kal´-sē-əm	**OXYGEN**	äk´-si-jən
CARBON DIOXIDE	kär´-bən dī-äk´sīd	**PREY**	prā
CARTILAGE	kär´-təl-ij	**PUPIL**	pyü-pəl
DENTICLE	dən´-ti-kəl	**RETINA**	re´-tən-ə
MUSCLE	mə´-səl	**SKELETON**	ske´-lə-tən
NERVE	nərv	**SPIRACLE**	spir´-i-kəl
NUTRIENT	nü´-trē-ˌənt	**YOLK**	yok
OPERCULUM	o´-pər-kyə-ləm		

ä as in c**a**rt ə as in b**a**nan**a** ü as in r**u**le

AMAZING SHARK FACTS

• The smallest kind of shark is probably the dwarf shark. It's usually about 25 centimeters long—small enough for a diver to hold easily in one hand. Take another look at the world's biggest kind of shark (page 15).

• The world's weirdest shark may be the goblin shark. It has a long snout that sticks out like a dagger above its beaklike upper jaw. Sawsharks are strange, too. They have a long, flat snout edged with needle-sharp teeth.

• Bull sharks sometimes swim up freshwater rivers. They have been found in the Amazon River, the Mississippi River, the Congo River, and others.

• Besides being able to taste with their mouths, sharks have taste-sensitive spots called pit organs all over their bodies. So in a way sharks can taste the water as they swim.

• Swell sharks got their name because of their special defensive tactic. When a swell shark is attacked, it swallows water and becomes too big for a predator to swallow easily.

GLOSSARY/INDEX

BONY FISH: Fish that have a skeleton of hard bone. **6, 9**

BRAIN: Body part that receives messages about what is happening inside and outside the body. The brain sends messages to put the body into action. **17–19, 21**

CALCIUM: Special material that makes bones hard and is added in layers to strengthen cartilage. **6, 7**

CARBON DIOXIDE: A waste gas that is given off by an animal's bodily activities. In fish, it is carried to the gills by the blood and passed out of the body. **29**

CARTILAGE: Lightweight, strong, rubbery material that forms a shark's skeleton. Layers of calcium make some parts even stronger. **6**

DENTICLES: Teethlike scales covering a shark's body. Like teeth, denticles are shed and replaced. **14, 32**

EAR: Body part that allows the shark to hear, to maintain balance, and to sense what direction it's swimming. **17**

EYE: Body part that lets the shark see. An opening, the pupil, gets bigger or smaller to control the amount of light entering. Then a lens focuses light on the retina, triggering signals that travel to the brain. **19–21, 23**

FIN: Body part that propels a shark through the water, helps it turn, or keeps it from rolling over. There are caudal, pectoral, pelvic, anal, and dorsal fins. **8–9, 27, 31**

GILL: Body part in which oxygen and carbon dioxide are exchanged, allowing fish to breathe. **4–5, 22, 25, 28–30**

GILL RAKER: Comblike part lining the inside of a fish's gills. In some, like basking sharks, gill rakers collect food particles called plankton. The plankton move into the shark's stomach when the shark swallows. **25**

HEART: Body part that acts like a pump, constantly pushing blood throughout the shark's body. **30**

INTESTINE: Body part in which special juices finish breaking food down into nutrients. **27**

LATERAL LINE: A long tube running down the sides of fish and connected to the surface by many short branches. Water movement causes motion inside this tube system. The motion is then detected by tiny hairs in the main tube, triggering signals that go to the brain. **21**

LIVER: Body part that cleans the blood. By storing body oils, it also helps buoy up the shark's body. **10**

MUSCLE: Body part that usually works in pairs. They move individual parts of the shark's skeleton by pulling on them from opposite sides. **15, 19, 22, 26, 30**

NASAL SAC: Body part containing folds of smell-sensitive tissue. The tissue detects odor particles in the water and sends signals to the brain. **18**

NERVES: Pathways that connect all parts of the shark's body to its brain. **17**

NUTRIENTS: Chemical building blocks into which food is broken down for use by the shark's body. The five basic nutrients provided by food are proteins, fats, carbohydrates, minerals, and vitamins. **27, 33**

OPERCULUM: The covering that protects gills of bony fish. **5**

OXYGEN: A gas in the air and water that is passed to the blood in the gills. Then the blood carries it throughout the shark's body. Oxygen is combined with food nutrients to produce energy to power muscles and other body functions. **5, 28–30, 33**

PREY: The food the shark catches and eats. **18–23**

RETINA: Layer at the back of the eye that is made up of light-sensitive cells. When light strikes the cells, messages are sent to the brain. The brain figures out these messages, and the shark sees. **19, 20**

SHELL GLAND: Special body part in most female sharks in which the male's sperm unites with the female's eggs. Then a baby shark develops. **31, 33**

SKELETON: The supporting framework that gives a body shape. **6–7, 15**

SPIRACLE: Opening found just behind the eye in many sharks. It lets water into the gills while the shark is eating. **28**

STOMACH: Body part in which special juices begin to break down food into small pieces that the shark uses for energy and growth. **25, 26**

SWIM BLADDER: Balloonlike body part that helps bony fish rise and sink. Sharks lack a swim bladder. **9**

TOOTH: Body part used for getting food. The tooth's shape is suited to what the shark eats. Several rows of teeth may be lost at one time, with more developing to replace any that are broken or lost. **11–14, 23**

YOLK: Food supply for some developing baby sharks. **31**

PHOTO CREDITS